JOY

JOY

Regardless of Circumstance

DILLON BRUCE

Foreword by MYRON BRUCE
Edited by EMILI TODD
Edited by MEGAN TIDWELL

Copyright © 2021 by Dillon Bruce

All rights reserved.

No part of this book may be reproduced in any form or by any electronic or mechanical means, including information storage and retrieval systems, without written permission from the author, except for the use of brief quotations in a book review.

This book is dedicated to my lovely wife, who reminds me of the reason we can all have joy, because I see Christ in her life!

To my mom, who for the early years of my life gave me an example of joy through her love for Christ.

To my grandma, who lovingly guided my thoughts and actions toward Christ throughout my years in college.

"Christians aren't consumers. We are contributors. We don't watch. We engage. We give. We sacrifice. We encourage. We do life together."

J. McNiell

"...my greatest fear is for those who sit in pews every Sunday and know nothing about true faith."

B. Edwards

Contents

Foreword	11
Why Joy?	13
1. JESUS	17
2. OTHERS	19
3. YOU	21
4. What is Joy?	23
5. The Source of Joy!	33
6. Feeling Joyful!	45
Notes	53
About the Author	55

Foreword

The apostle John said it best as he wrote 3rd John chapter 1, verse 4:

> *"I have no greater joy than this, to hear of my children walking in the truth."*

Certainly, he was referring to Gaius in verse one as well as other faithful children of God. Yet it's true that the same is applicable for me as I consider the author of this book. Dillon is joining an exceptional group of professionals as he turns both his mind and pen to expressing his heart in the written word. Demonstrating a desire to inspire the reader to live a life of JOY comes as no surprise to those who know him. Just as he has already blessed many in the ministry, I am thankful he has chosen this method to motivate hundreds of thousands more. Those who know Dillon will see his JOYFUL heart within these pages. Weaving God's word into our daily lives is how we come to know and experience true JOY. This book is a quick read and one that will spur you on to consider ways you will not only feel JOY in your life but bring JOY to others. It is truly a topic about which Dillon is capable of writing, and it is, undeniably appropriate for a time such as this!

- Myron Bruce

Why Joy?

Why are you reading a book about joy? Is there something you're missing that keeps joy from overflowing out of your life? Sadly, this is exactly why I wrote this book, because I've experienced too many conversations with people who are missing out on a joyful life. Joy is something every person can have if they look to the right source.

On January 4th, 2020, I married my beautiful wife. Yes, the year of Covid-19 started with our wedding. Two weeks later I started my first job right out of college, working for the Keller church of Christ in Keller, TX as the Education Minister. What we were told would be the honeymoon phase of our marriage became a rollercoaster of life! Over the course of the next year we endured THREE historical events in our lives, two of which could very well end up in future history books that our kids might read! It was at this moment I realized... people need joy. To put it even more simply, people need the Lord. I hope this book brings you joy and helps you understand why joy is accessible and available to any and everyone!

If you want to know the secret to joy,
it is...

1

JESUS

JESUS

IS

FIRST.

2

OTHERS

OTHERS

ARE

SECOND.

3

YOU

YOU

ARE

LAST.

4

What is Joy?

The simplest way to describe joy is Jesus, Others, Yourself. We actually read of this throughout the Gospel accounts! Matt. 22:34-40,

> *"But when the Pharisees heard that he had silenced the Sadducees, they gathered together. And one of them, a lawyer, asked him a question to test him. "Teacher, which is the great commandment in the Law?" And he said to him, "You shall love the Lord your*

God with all your heart and with all your soul and with all your mind. This is the great and first commandment. And a second is like it: You shall love your neighbor as yourself. On these two commandments depend all the Law and the Prophets." [1]

DIRECTLY FROM THE MOUTH OF Christ we read that the greatest command is to love God, and the second is to love others. Here, Jesus is quoting from the old law[2] and is telling us how we should obey God and how we can inherit eternal life. Christ literally gives the key to life! The first step is putting God first. The second step is putting others second.

There are two distinct ways we can look at these commands. For the first command; if we love God and have made Him number one in our life, then everything we do will be done because of our love for God. If I pray and read my Bible, I do that because I love God.

What is Joy?

If I am a good steward of the things I've been given, I do that because I love God. Therefore, the reason I do anything good in life is because I love God! That's why this is the greatest command... because God should be number one in our lives and also because it contains all other commands within it.

Now what about the second greatest? Isn't it contained within the first command? Don't I show compassion, mercy, and love for my neighbors because I love God? Absolutely! However, there is another point we can gain from this second command. If God is first above all else, and your neighbor is next, then there is nowhere else for you to be except last. This seems like a great start to telling folks they can have a joyful life, am I right? "I'm looking for joy and you're telling me that I am last. Also, Jesus and everyone else should be regarded as greater than me?" That's exactly right! Before we even start exploring what a life filled with joy looks like, we have to understand it begins by putting ourselves last.

This command is so frequent in scripture as well! Christ said, *"The last will be first, and the first last."* (Matt. 20:16). We are told over and over we must be humble, but once again, how does that bring ME joy!? I just want to feel that sense of JOY! The problem might be right there. In order to have joy, your goal cannot be to find it for yourself alone. Joy is tricky that way. When you seek it for self-satisfaction, you'll never find it. When you *"seek first the kingdom of God"* (Matt. 6:33) then you will be filled with joy. That's what I mean by Jesus, Others, Yourself. It's amazing that Christ tells us exactly how we can have joy and be filled with this inexpressible feeling.

In fact, the amazing thing is that Christ told us how we can be filled with joy a couple thousand years before doctors began to understand this reality. A few years ago, a group of psychologists supported by the University of

Michigan and Seattle Pacific University published a research article in which they examined the goal of putting others first (described in their study as "compassionate goals") and the effect it had on those with severe anxiety and depression. Their published study is outlined below.

"Objective

Interpersonal models of depression and anxiety have not examined the role of interpersonal goals in shaping relationships and symptoms. Striving to promote/protect desired self-images (self-image goals) may undermine relationships and increase symptoms, whereas striving to support others (compassionate goals) may be protective, but clinical relevance is unknown.

Method

We tested effects of compassionate versus self-image goals on interpersonal functioning and symptoms in clinically depressed and/or anxious participants (N = 47) during 10 days of experience sampling, over a 6-week follow-up, and in a dyadic relationship.

Results

Participants reported higher conflict and symptoms on days that they most pursued self-image goals, but noted higher perceived support and lower symptoms when pursuing compassionate goals. Goals prospectively predicted symptom changes 6 weeks later. Lastly, informant-rated interpersonal goals predicted relationship satisfaction of both patients and significant others.

Conclusion

Results suggest the relevance of self-image and compassionate goals for the interpersonal maintenance of depression and anxiety." [3]

What is Joy?

Joy can be most simply described as 1, 2, 3... Jesus, You and Me.

We recognize joy in others when we see it, so why does it seem so hard to grasp? If I know I should put Jesus first, everyone else next, and myself last, then why is it so hard to have this ever so coveted joy? This was the problem for the rich young man who came to Jesus in Mark chapter 10. He was choosing to put Jesus first and came to Him and said, "What must I do to inherit eternal life?" Jesus starts by telling him the same thing He told the lawyer in Matthew chapter 22, to love God and love others. When the rich young man explains he has kept all those commandments from his youth, Jesus then raises the bar. He tells him to go, sell all of his possessions and give them to the poor. Upon hearing this, the rich young man went away sad because he couldn't give up the things he held onto so dearly. Even though he had sought out Jesus, wanted to put Jesus first and was looking to obey Jesus, he still went away sad because there was something else more important in his life than Jesus. The Lord knew what it was this rich young man held close to his heart, so that was the exact thing Jesus told him to let go - his possessions.

Many of us face this exact problem today! You may seek out Christ, be willing to put Him first and want to obey what He says. Then Jesus says to you, "Give up ___ in order to follow me." This may be different for each person. For the rich young man, it was his possessions. For us, it may be possessions, money, power, popularity, recognition, family, country, sports, school, career - you name it. There are so many things that keep us from fully being dedicated to Christ. If you were to put yourself in the position of the rich young man in Mark 10, what would Jesus ask you to remove from your life? Would you be able to remove it without hesitation, or would you honestly go away sad because you know you cannot rid your life of certain things? It is easy to say "Jesus is first."

However, when we are face to face with the decision to choose Christ over things of this world, it is easier said than done. This is the root of joy - choosing Christ no matter what. When Jesus is first and things in life go south, then you will still have joy. Why? For this reason: Jesus. Never. Changes. No matter what sour things happen in our lives on this earth, we can still have joy through complete reliance on Christ. Joy is not reliant on the things around you, because joy is available regardless of circumstances.

5

The Source of Joy!

We've established that true joy comes from Christ alone, but how do we get this joy from Him if He walked the earth 2000 years ago? How do we tap into the joy that He is offering? We know the source, but now we need to dive head first into the well of living water! How?

> *"And behold, I am with you always, to the end of the age."*
> Matt. 28:20

> *"Keep your life free from the love of money, and be content with what you have, for he has said, 'I will never leave you nor forsake you.'"* Heb. 13:5

> *"For I am sure that neither death nor life, nor angels nor rulers, nor things present nor things to come, nor powers, nor height nor depth, nor anything else in all creation, will be able to separate us from the love of God in Christ Jesus our Lord."* Rom. 8:38-39

TOO OFTEN CHRISTIANS AROUND the world find themselves waiting for Christ; waiting for Him to make the move and show us He is here with us. The truth is, Christ is so close, that He can even hear the quietest whisper loud and clear. The amazing thing is that no matter what we do, He will never leave us! He is the source of everything good and just. From Him comes love, truth, righteousness, and JOY! This joy, unlike simple happiness that comes and goes, does not depend on any external circumstances! It's that simple! The source of our joy is right in front of us! Our job is to dive in head first. When we realize who Christ is and what He's offering, we have to simply ask ourselves, 'is the happiness the world might bring worth more than the joy Christ brings?'

Paul explained this in great detail in Philippians chapter 4.

> *"I rejoiced in the Lord greatly that now at length you have revived your concern for me. You were indeed concerned for me, but you had no opportunity. Not that I am speaking of being in need, for I have learned in whatever situation I am to be content. I know how to be brought low, and I know how to abound. In any and every circumstance, I have learned the secret of facing plenty and hunger,*

> *abundance and need. I can do all things through Him who strengthens me."* Philippians 4:10-13

The point is that the joy found in Christ is not dependent on any other circumstances of life. You can almost imagine the church in Philippi on the edge of their seats as this letter from Paul is being read to them. The phrase, "I have learned the secret..." will make anyone sit up, sit forward, and hang on each word that follows. The secret is in Christ. I can make it through everything, I can be content through everything, I can do all things, I CAN HAVE JOY, through Him who strengthens me!

Another thing we need to direct our attention towards, concerning the source of joy, is the sharing of joy. In Paul's letter to Philemon, Paul encouraged him by mentioning all the great things that Philemon had done. Paul mentions in verse 7 of his letter to Philemon, that he had "refreshed the hearts of the saints" by his love! Paul even said that this gave him "joy and comfort!" Further on in verse 20, Paul actually asks Philemon to "refresh my heart!" Now as we think about Philemon refreshing the saints through love, we direct attention to Matthew chapter 11. In verse 28, Jesus says,

> *"Come to Me, all who are weary and heavy-laden, and I will give you rest."*

That word *rest* in the Greek is **anapauo,**[1] also translated as *refresh* or *refreshed*, which is the same word Paul used in his letter to Philemon. What did Paul say about Philemon refreshing the saints? That it brought him JOY and comfort! When we come to Christ and find our rest in Christ, He brings us joy and comfort! Perhaps my favorite part of all is this, not only can we all find our rest in Christ, but we can also share the joy and comfort we have in Christ with everyone, just as Philemon did! All people can find rest in Christ!

All people can be refreshed, **_anapauo_**, by one another! All people can have joy right now! It all starts at the Source of joy, comfort and rest. It starts with Jesus of Nazareth, the Christ, the Son of the living God! This is how you dive in head first into the living water.

Just as Peter confessed,

> *"You are the Christ, the Son of the living God."* Matt. 16:16

Or as John stated,

> *"Behold, the Lamb of God, who takes away the sin of the world!"* John 1:29

Or as the centurion and other Roman soldiers with him said,

> *"Truly this was the Son of God!"* Matt. 27:54

Now, if you think you can confess Christ, move on with life, and not make any changes to your life, that could not be further from the truth. Those who expect eternal salvation and joy in this life, based only on words that are said, do not understand the whole picture. Believing in and confessing Jesus as the Son of God is just the beginning of all things related to your spiritual life, not the end of it. Jesus makes this clear in Matthew 7:21-23 as He says,

> *"Not everyone who says to me, 'Lord, Lord,' will enter the kingdom of heaven, but the one who does the will of my Father who is in heaven. On that day many will say to me, 'Lord, Lord, did we not prophesy in your name, and cast out demons in your name, and do many mighty works in your name?' And I will declare to them, 'I never knew you; depart from me, you workers of lawlessness.'"*

Upon confession of Christ as the Son of the living God, there must be a change that takes place, there is a change of commitment. When you believe in something, you are committed to it. However, the term "believe" has been so watered down in our culture, that even the words of Christ Himself are misunderstood when He states in John 3:16,

> "For God so loved the world, that He gave his only Son, that whoever believes in Him should not perish but have eternal life."

When He says, "that whoever believes" it does not mean to just call upon the name of the Lord. It does not mean to just "accept" Him as your savior. That is the exact opposite of what he said in Matthew 7! Other translations even say in John 3:16, "Every person who commits himself to Jesus will not be destroyed." [2] The point Jesus is making here is not to simply say, "I believe! Now I'm good!", but instead to center your life around Him! To commit your life to Him.

- When Jesus says to believe in Him, that means we must give Him our whole heart.
- We cannot give Him our whole heart, if we are not committed.
- We cannot commit, if we do not change our lives.
- We cannot change our lives, if we don't realize the need for Christ and obey Him.

It can be said many times, "I believe", but true belief in Christ happens through the way we live our lives. True belief happens when we choose to obey Him in word and deed. As James put it,

> *"But be doers of the word, and not hearers only, deceiving yourselves. For if anyone is a hearer of the word and not a doer, he is like a man who looks intently at his natural*

> *face in the mirror. For he looks at himself and goes away and at once forgets what he was like. But the one who looks into the perfect law, the law of liberty, and perseveres, being no hearer who forgets but a doer who acts, he will be blessed in his doing."* James 1:22-25

It really boils down to a heart issue. Everyone must ask themselves, "is my heart with Christ?" Otherwise, you might just be crying out, "Lord, Lord."

THIS IS THE SOURCE OF JOY. JESUS Christ of Nazareth, the Son of the living God. The Lamb of God who takes away the sin of the world. Confessing your belief in Him, making the decision to be committed to Him in all things, and obeying His commands of being born of water and the Spirit (John 3). Just as Jesus told Nicodemus, "You must be born again", we also must be born again. That's exactly why salvation in Christ doesn't just depend on words that are said, but rather, obedience! When you are baptized for the forgiveness of your sins, you are obeying the commandment laid out in scripture. It is simply responding to a promise of forgiveness, and that promise is for everyone. Every person who makes this decision will have joy, now (in a moment of rejoicing) and for eternity (in the presence on God)!

6

Feeling Joyful!

Singing spreads joy!

66 *"Shout hallelujah! Shout hallelujah! Shout hallelujah unto the Lord! Sing aloud to God, let the people shout before His throne hallelujah! Sing aloud to God, make a joyful noise unto the Lord!"* [1]

IT IS HARD TO DENY THAT SINGING spreads joy! To quote Buddy the Elf, "The best way to spread Christmas cheer, is singing loud for all to hear!" Singing is, by far, the best way to let people know you are full of joy. When you are singing praises to God, and when you always have a song on your heart, it's impossible not to be joyful. Just as we can refresh one another by our love (Philemon 7), we can also refresh one another with our voices. Children understand this very well when they sing,

> *"I've got the joy, joy, joy, joy down in my heart! And I'm so happy, so very happy! I've got the love of Jesus in my heart!"*

When you sing this song, happiness is poured out and it refreshes those around you! Songs are also a reminder of Who is in control, Who sits on the throne, and in Whom our joy is found!

> *"In Christ alone my hope is found, He is my light, my strength, my song. This Cornerstone, this solid*

Ground, firm through the fiercest drought and storm. What heights of love, what depths of peace. When fears are stilled, when strivings cease. My Comforter, my All in All, here in the love of Christ I stand!" ²

There is a reason we're instructed in scripture to sing. When we put words to music, it causes us to meditate and think on them in a deeper way. We do this by saying them "louder and longer while moving our voices up and down!" It's a way to share and show Christ in our lives. Paul and Silas set this example for us while they were in prison,

> *"About midnight Paul and Silas were praying and singing hymns to God, and the prisoners were listening to them..."* Acts 16:25

The prisoners were listening to them! If we continue reading through verse 26 and following, we learn that even the jailer and his entire family were converted to Christ. Singing not only encourages us to set our minds on God, but it is a tool we use to share Christ.

Think about the character I mentioned above, Buddy the Elf. He is Joy personified! Nothing really gets him down, he always sings, is always smiling, and seeks to improve other people's lives. Now, he does this for the sake of Christmas, but I want you to think about the joy Buddy brought to all and ask yourself, "Can I do this (personify joy) for the sake of Christ?" Can I carry on in song? Can I remember to give hugs and brighten everyone's day? Can I wear a smile wherever I go? I'll go ahead and answer the question for you. YES! Yes, you can do all of this. You can wear joy, like it's your wedding band you never take off. It's not a matter of - if you can? It's just a matter of - **if you will?**

> "My life's in You, my strength's in You, my hope's in You. In You, it's in You." [3]

This is why you can sing, smile, hug, and wear joy like a wedding band; because your life, hope, and strength are all in Christ! When you die to your old life and begin your new life in Christ, it is a lifelong commitment to live for Him. You are making a commitment to wear a wedding band that shows you belong to Christ. Just as husbands and wives show their commitment to each other through the ring on their finger, we show our commitment to Christ through the way we live our lives. Can anyone be committed to Christ and not show joy? Can anyone be committed to Christ and not spread joy?!

Once again, there is a difference between joy and happiness. Some people will say we cannot always control how we feel and that we can't always make ourselves feel happy. That is exactly right, you cannot control your happiness! We feel happy when good things happen and sad when bad things happen. However, joy is available to everyone regardless of circumstance! We can, and should, choose to seek Christ for the source of our strength. When we choose Christ, we are choosing joy. Therefore, joy doesn't rely on good circumstances, but rather on Christ alone. Joy is simply filling your life with Christ, no longer having a list of priorities, since He is the only commitment. When you are filled with Christ, He brings joy to your life and the lives around you.

This book was written because I realized so many people were searching for joy and calling it happiness. So many people want that feeling of joy, and they assume it's found in material things, much like happiness. True joy is only found in Christ, the Son of the Living God. It's available to anyone regardless of the circumstances in one's life! You can choose Christ right now and center your life around Him. Then you will be amazed at the joy that follows! When Christ is at the center of your life, your joy will not go away because you know without a shadow of a doubt that your Savior is the one who sits on the eternal heavenly throne.

Notes

4. What is Joy?

1. All scripture is from the ESV translation.
2. Deut. 6:5 & Lev. 19:18
3. For more information about this study: https://onlinelibrary.wiley.com/doi/abs/10.1002/jc...

5. The Source of Joy!

1. Check biblestudytools.com for more study on greek in the NT.
2. The IEB Study Bible Translation

6. Feeling Joyful!

1. "Shout Hallelujah": Gill, Randy Copyright 2003
2. "In Christ Alone": Stuart Townend & Keith Getty Copyright © 2001
3. "My Life Is In You": Daniel Gardner Copyright 1999

About the Author

I grew up at Waterview Church of Christ in Richardson, TX. After high school graduation in May of 2016 I went on to Freed-Hardeman University where I spent 3.5 years and received my Bachelor's in Biblical Studies. I got married to my beautiful wife in January of 2020 (yes we began our life together in what most people consider to be the worst year ever), then I began working for the Keller Church of Christ 2 weeks later. I have been continuing the work as the Education Minister at Keller Church of Christ since then. I love the Church and I love working for the Church! In addition to working for Keller, I am the Co-Host of The Bible Conversations Podcast. Connect with me today on social media!

Made in the USA
Columbia, SC
07 May 2024